Too Simple for Words

Reflections on Non-Duality

Too Simple for Words

Reflections on Non-Duality

Graham Stew

BOOKS

Winchester, UK
Washington, USA

First published by O-Books, 2016
O-Books is an imprint of John Hunt Publishing Ltd., Laurel House, Station Approach,
Alresford, Hants, SO24 9JH, UK
office1@jhpbooks.net
www.johnhuntpublishing.com

For distributor details and how to order please visit the 'Ordering' section on our website.

Text copyright: Graham Stew 2015

ISBN: 978 1 78535 271 3
Library of Congress Control Number: 2015949724

A CIP catalogue record for this book is available from the British Library.

Design: Stuart Davies

Printed and bound by CPI Group (UK) Ltd, Croydon, CR0 4YY, UK

We operate a distinctive and ethical publishing philosophy in all
areas of our business, from our global network of authors to
production and worldwide distribution.

CONTENTS

To Lana

Foreword

Another book on non-duality? What's the point of all these words? It's all been written already... by those with greater insight and command of language. Besides, words are extremely limited in expressing these matters. Words divide, separate and complicate. They use 'subjects' and 'objects' and are inevitably dualistic.

Words refer to 'things'... and Truth or the Absolute is not a thing. It is that which contains things... It is the capacity within which things (thoughts, feelings, sensations) arise and pass away.

So, words are intrinsically misleading and ultimately useless. What else do we have to communicate with? Silence. Actions. Non-action. Smiling. Laughter. Loving. All these are sufficient and eloquent enough.

Words are only pointers; never the 'thing itself'. The word 'water' is not wet and cannot relieve thirst. The word is not real, but can be mistaken for the real, such is our dependence upon language. In this book I shall have to use the convention of language, using personal pronouns and subject/object forms in a mixture of reflections and dialogues. I shall also use capital letters to indicate the Real (Absolute; Truth; Oneness; God; whatever word we may use to indicate Reality). There will inevitably be some repetition for which I do not apologise; the repetition of the same message in different ways can often aid understanding.

So I ask the reader to take my words as mere signposts... to savour them... as one would taste unknown food, or listen to new music. Let the meaning resonate where it will... some insight may be gained; some questions answered; and new questions prompted. Look beyond the words, beyond the mind... which will never, ever 'get' this... as it's too simple for words!

Graham Stew

Just who do you think you are?

We all seem to have a good story to tell about ourselves... the story of our life. It's a tale that has been refined and developed and nurtured for as long as we can remember. Our parents gave us a name, and from thereon we gained a sense of being a separate person. From about the age of two we sensed that the world 'out there' was an alien and potentially hostile place, and that our bodies were sources of pleasure and pain. Language developed and its dualistic nature emphasised the division between self and 'other'. 'Subject' and 'object' were born. Identity became increasingly important throughout our early school years... the concepts of 'me' and 'mine' featuring more frequently in our contact with the world.

Along with name came gender, possessions, likes and dislikes, abilities and weaknesses... the need to compare ourselves with others. All these reinforced the developing self-image... the evolving personality. It is worth noting that the word personality is derived from the Greek *'persona'*, the megaphone-like mask worn by actors. It is this 'mask' of selfhood which we have worn and protected all our lives; this conceptual wall behind which we have sheltered and from which we have addressed the 'outside world'.

The message of this book is that this separation of the person from the world is essentially false... our sense of self is a tragic mistake, and is the cause of all our problems. This message may not be apparent, and may also be resisted by the ego, the little self which desperately maintains its separateness in order to exist. Throughout this book I shall return to this basic question... and invite you to investigate just who you think you really are.

When asked this question we often think of the story of our life, don't we? There is that television programme called *Who Do You Think You Are?* which consists of certain celebrities tracing their family trees back over many generations. This involves uncovering the dramatic, fascinating and often moving stories of their parents, grandparents, and so on. Is that all we are then… a story that we tell ourselves (*and others… if they ask*)? A collection of memories of events; a mixture of experiences, perceived as either positive or negative? A unique story of course, resulting in the personality you have today, with the blend of experiences, opinions and values, hopes and fears that mark you out as an individual. But… just a story?

As a simple exercise can I suggest that you take a piece of paper and a pen, and ask yourself the question, "Who am I?" Now write down 20 answers to that question (or as many as you can manage).

Once you have finished look down through your list of answers. You may have mentioned your name, age, nationality and things like: sister/brother, daughter/son, wife/husband, job, religious or political affiliations, and so on. Now go through your list and cross out any answer that could possibly apply to someone else. That will certainly include answers like daughter/son, and may even include your name. What answer is left? Is there anything about 'you' that is unique? You have answered "me" or "my experience". Are you referring to that collection of memories and concepts which make up your sense of individuality? Isn't this the story of yourself referred to earlier? The story that I wish to explore in this book. In the pages to come I shall ask you to be resolute and uncompromising in searching out the truth about this story, its consequences and its implications.

Are you your body?

Let's take this investigation one step at a time, and use our intellect to explore these questions in a scientific and systematic manner. There will come a point when the mind can go no further into these matters, and we will recognise the limits of our intelligence (as well as the illusion of any belief system). Until then, let me guide you through a series of questions.

We normally talk of 'having' a body, rather than being a body. If you have a body, where do you situate yourself in relation to it? Where do you visualise yourself? Are you in your head? In the brain? Do you see yourself located in the heart? If you lose part of your body, for example through an amputation of a limb, are you less of a person? More than one limb? How much of your body could you lose and still remain essentially 'you'? When your hair or fingernails are cut, are you diminishing as a person?

Where do 'you' end, and the 'world outside' begin? When you breathe in, does the oxygen that enters your body become part of you? When you go to the toilet, does part of you get flushed away? When you eat a cheese sandwich is that now what you are? Are we not continuously exchanging elements, liquids and gases with our environment? The boundary between 'you' and the external world becomes increasingly blurred the more you investigate these questions.

The reality is that there is an *interdependence* between the world and our bodies... one cannot exist without the other... they arise mutually. Consisting of the four elements of earth, air, fire and water, all material things are continuously created and destroyed. Our bodies, value and protect them as we may, are no exception. Our bodies will age, become diseased, and die... that is inescapable fact. It is an unpalatable fact for most people, who would rather not think about this, let alone discuss it. However, if we face these fears and look closely into them, the interdependence of all living things indicates that there is no real separation... all differences and distinctions are imaginary... the products of our minds.

Let me ask again... are you your body? If you '*have*' a body... then it's obvious that you are *other* than a body. May I invite you to carry out another simple exercise? Close your eyes, and then ask yourself... "Where does my body end and the world begin?"

Where are the boundaries between 'self' and 'other'? Take your time to really sense this boundary… can you find it? Of course there are sensations coming from the body that you recognise as 'me'… but actually where they are being sensed? Isn't there simply awareness of touch, sounds, smells… input from all the senses… being received in awareness? An infinitely empty awareness… a still and vast spaciousness in which everything appears. Open your eyes, and visual stimuli flood into awareness… and you start to watch the world *'out there'*. But in fact isn't the world appearing *in* what you are… the presence-awareness that you **really** are?

So we can say that we have a body – but do we have any control over it? The heart is beating, the stomach and intestines are digesting food, blood is circulating oxygen to the tissues, white blood cells are destroying harmful bacteria… who does this? Don't these processes simply happen? If you think you are controlling any of these functions, then just try to stop breathing for five minutes! If we had control over our bodies, would we ever choose to catch a cold, or develop a disease, or even age and die? Is it not true that our body appears in our awareness, undergoes changes, and that these changes are witnessed by us. This witnessing is evidence that we are NOT our bodies; leaving us with the inevitable question: "If I am not my body… then what or who am I?"

Let us keep exploring… ever deeper.

Are you your sensations?

What are you aware of right now? Open up your awareness to all your five senses. Right now, what is happening?

Over here, there is awareness of –

Church bells; birdsong; bees humming; dogs barking… hearing is happening.

Tea and toast… tasting is happening.

Roses and chocolate cake… smelling is happening.

The typing on the computer screen… seeing is happening.

The warmth of the sun; the softness of the cushion in my back… touching is happening.

'I' am not doing anything… everything is just happening… coming into awareness and passing away… a natural flow of being.

So what is happening where 'you' are? Right now… what is being sensed? Work through all five senses – hearing, smelling, tasting, seeing, touching… note what is being sensed. Now notice that the space in which these things are happening is what 'you' truly are. That spacious awareness in which all these sensations are arising is what 'you' are. 'You' are not doing the seeing… doing the hearing; seeing and hearing and everything else are just happening… unfolding right now in that presence and awareness.

Notice also the continuous change of sensations. Nothing stays still… all is changing. A continual arising and passing away of sensations… and an awareness of these sensations. If you are this awareness, the sensations must be 'other' than you. So, are you your sensations?

Are you your thoughts and feelings?

It's the same with thoughts and feelings. What exactly are they? An individual might have up to 70,000 thoughts a day… but where do they come from, and where do they go? Some thoughts may have an emotional 'charge' or flavour and we call these feelings or emotions; but are they different in nature from thoughts? Some thoughts are powerful and capture our attention immediately with an emotional 'kick', and then take us away on a mental journey… on a train of thought. We arrive, sometimes minutes later, 'somewhere else' in our heads, not remembering how we got there… such is the power of thought, if we give it the energy of our attention. What else is the mind apart from thoughts? The mind consists of ideas, concepts, perceptions, meanings, opinions, memories… all mental activities covered by the term 'thinking'.

All of us can recall lying awake in bed at night wishing the mind had an 'off' switch, because thoughts were keeping us wide awake. Often these thoughts are accompanied by uncomfortable feelings – anxiety, depression, fear, anger and so on. There is no peace in the mind. Its nature is restlessness. The mind is a machine designed for thinking. As a problem-solver it is wonderfully useful… we need it to earn our living, pay our bills, etc… Without the mind, we would not have penicillin and the marvels of modern medicine. Neither would we have the nuclear bombs and poison gas. The mind has no inherent morality… that is a human addition.

You may feel that you *are* your mind, and that you control your thoughts. If that were the case wouldn't you choose only to experience pleasant thoughts, and not have worries and negative emotions? Do you know what your next thought will be? If I were to ask you not to think about a blue table (for example) for five minutes… could you? Isn't it true that you don't know what your next thought will be… or where it comes from… or where it goes? Perhaps thoughts are simply waves of electrical energy within the brain, which acts as some kind of transmitter/receiver? But that's just another thought too!

As a simple exercise, spend a few moments now quietly watching your thoughts… just observe them arising and passing away. Focus attention on whatever appears, as if you are a cat watching a mouse hole. Note with interest whatever comes up, but then let it go… don't get caught up in any sequence of thinking. You can certainly feed your thoughts by giving them attention; they then grow in force and often bring emotions and physical sensations with them. Just notice how fear or anger feels in your body if it arises. Note what's present now… and now… and again now.

Did you get a sense of the stream of thoughts that are continually arising? Were you able to simply watch them float by without getting tangled up with them? If you are aware of thoughts, you cannot *be* them, can you? That is logical isn't it? Being able to watch your thoughts means you must be *other* than them. You are the **awareness** in which thoughts and feelings arise and pass away… just like all your sensations. The screen of awareness remains untouched by the sensations, thoughts and feelings projected upon it. That awareness is what **you** are.

In the midst of winter
the garden quiet and cold,
and a rose still smiling.

Waking, Dreaming and Dreamless Sleep

Traditionally, three states of being have been identified for all humans: waking, dreaming, and dreamless sleep. Let's examine each of them in turn. We are all familiar with being awake... or are we? Does this level of consciousness vary? Physiologically, consciousness does fluctuate, and is affected by such factors as fatigue, drugs, alcohol, mental illness and fever. Being aware, here and now, of what is arising in consciousness, and being able to function in the world, are characteristics of wakefulness.

We may be awake for two-thirds of our lives, but without sleep for the other third, we would not survive. Deprived of sleep, we become delirious, hallucinate, lose our sanity and die. Dreaming, or REM (rapid eye movement) sleep, can resemble the waking state remarkably. We sense, think and feel our way through all types of adventurous and dramatic dreams; the only difference is that we remain in our beds. We may dream that our house is on fire, but on waking in a sweaty panic, we realise immediately that we have been dreaming, and would not for a moment contemplate calling the fire brigade. Dreams are simply a different state of consciousness, still full of mental activity, yet not registering fully in our memory. Many people attribute special significance to dreams, and spend a great deal of energy in interpreting them. This is nonsense. The parade of thoughts, feelings and sensations in dreams has no more ultimate reality or meaning than our 'waking dreams'. They are simply phenomena arising and disappearing within awareness. Using the mind to try to understand the mind seems pointless and absurd.

It is dreamless sleep that is vital to our mental and physical health. In these periods of deep sleep, it is as if consciousness is on 'stand-by' for an unusual noise might wake us immediately. In dreamless sleep there is no recorded mental activity; the mind has shut down. Without the functioning of the mind, there is no perception of time or space… there is nothing. It is this 'nothingness' that recharges us; paradoxically this emptiness fills us again. We are connected again to our Source. When we wake in the morning we know if we have had a restful night's sleep by the periods of 'absence' we have enjoyed. What bliss it is, when we are tired, to relax into the spacious emptiness that is our natural state! In letting go of our consciousness, we 'die' each night; so why should this relief be feared so much? For the ego, non-existence is the ultimate horror.

A December sky
Seagulls flying... somewhere...
Do they know?

Awareness

Right now, as you read these words, you ARE. Can you doubt this fact in any way? It is undeniable that 'you' (*whatever that is*) exist. There is aliveness, Being, and awareness. Even if you deny this fact, the very denial demonstrates that *something* is aware! We will explore the nature of that awareness later, but let's first accept the obvious fact that 'you' are aware. This awareness can be regarded as the screen or backdrop on which every sensation, thought and feeling is projected. Like the TV or cinema screen which remains untouched by whatever is projected upon it, this awareness is the empty *potential* or *possibility* for whatever arises. A TV screen can contain and convey all types of scenes... tragic, comic, exciting, dull... but its actual nature never changes. Once the programmes have ceased transmission, the screen remains... empty and silent (*as in deep sleep*).

Everything appears in this awareness... all objects, ideas, concepts, and perceptions. They arise, appear on the screen of awareness, and then disappear. We don't know where they came from, and we don't know where they go. We can't tell what our next thought or sensation is going to be, so the assumption of being in control of our minds requires a closer look. Thoughts arise and pass away... thinking happens... without the need for a 'thinker'. Awareness (*which is what we really **are***) accepts everything without discrimination or judgment. Whatever phenomena arise make no impression on awareness and they all pass away. Nothing stays the same... everything changes – except Awareness, which is timeless and without characteristics of any kind. Anything that can be said about awareness is conceptual, and only appears on the screen of this consciousness as a passing thought. Awareness is non-conceptual, and therefore cannot be defined, described, or known. Consequently, the mind (which arises in awareness) will never comprehend awareness (which contains the mind). Conceptual thinking can neither apprehend nor comprehend the non-conceptual.

The world is a verb.
There are no nouns… no objects.
The world is 'worlding'.
Trees are 'treeing'… birds are 'birding'
People are 'peopling'
The Self is 'Selfing'.

Duality

The mind is a wonderful machine for thinking, labelling, classifying, judging and problem-solving. We need our minds to function in everyday life, but let's see 'mind' for what it really is. The nature of mind consists of thoughts and perceptions constantly arising and passing away... there is nothing permanent or stable about the mind. Because what is Real never changes and is outside time, mind cannot be regarded as anything real. What we call memories provide an impression of duration and a personal history, but they are merely transitory mental activity being perceived Now. Memories are present perceptions of an imaginary past.

The other important aspect of mind is that it is essentially dualistic. It divides, compares and contrasts. Thought has created the opposites of: inside and outside, up and down, black and white, good and bad... etc. We assume and judge according to these pairs of opposites, these judgments harden into a burden of opinions, values and views which are carried around with us, and provide an illusory sense of personal identity. We label ourselves as poor... and want to be rich; as unhappy... and want to be happy; as lost... and want to be found. We spend our lives liking and disliking (*foods, people, countries, religions, etc.*), unaware that these distinctions are nothing more than mental constructs.

Before thought arises to differentiate, there are no distinctions in awareness... there is simply This (*and not even that!*).

Breathing happening
Thinking happening…
the usual show.

Suffering and Happiness

We suffer because we believe ourselves to be separate beings. This mistaken sense of 'self' and 'other' is the root of all our problems. It is the duality of thought which creates this division, where naturally there is none. There is only This, right here and now… in all its apparent diversity and true Oneness. Because we desire things to be other than they are, seeking arises. This results in suffering. We want things that we don't have, and don't want things that we do have. As soon as one desire is satisfied… whether it's food, sex, worldly success or material possessions… the desire for something new arises. The satisfaction of desire provides us with a sense of temporary fulfilment and peace, but it is short-lived. We seem to live in continuous states of desire and aversion, seeking contentment somewhere else and in something else. It might be a new job, car, house, or partner… or even freedom from seeking – so-called 'liberation' or 'enlightenment'. However, the very act of seeking prolongs the idea that there is someone who can get something, and also prolongs the desire for things to be other than they are. A most vicious circle.

In the course of labelling all phenomena, we assume there is a state called 'happiness', which we do not currently enjoy. Is happiness to be found or gained? Isn't happiness the absence of desire? Most of our lives are filled with desire, aren't they? Wanting this… not wanting that. All of these desires are wishing for something other than what IS. We experience transient and superficial happiness if we are given something we have desired: new clothes, bigger car, better house, new job, new partner. Even something as subtle as making 'spiritual progress' is a source of satisfaction for the ego. The removal of desire leads to happiness… and happiness is our true nature. Life at its essence is pure naked JOY… and we cover it over with our trivial and egocentric desires. Drop them all… fall in love with what you have now… with what IS… and happiness will naturally arise. For no one!

Is it possible to live without desire? To be completely content with things as they are? To accept whatever comes along with equanimity and gratitude? Perhaps… if there is an exploration of the nature of suffering. There may arise an understanding of why suffering occurs… and then the question "Who suffers?" can be addressed. If, as we have already learned, we are not our body, thoughts or feelings… and if we can really SEE that truth, then who is there to suffer, even if unpleasant thoughts and sensations arise? We spend our lives looking in the wrong places for happiness, when true happiness is always right here, inside us. We overlook the fact that our true nature is Happiness… all the joy and peace we seek is ours already.

The world wants to sleep in winter,
Thoughts keep it awake...
Put the kettle on.

Time and Space

When is now? Can there be ever a time other than Now? We can only live in this present moment… think, feel, remember, plan… Now. It is outside of time… and so cannot even be called eternal. Mind has created time in order to organise thought, and invent an illusory succession of events… seemingly to prevent everything from happening at once (which it actually does – wonderfully, spontaneously!). But I hear you saying: "*What about my life… has that been an illusion?*" In an absolute sense… yes. Your memories of your past are recalled in the present. You remember the so-called past now. It exists in your awareness now. You may be planning a holiday in the future… but that planning and anticipation is happening now. You may remember last year's holiday, but those memories are happening now.

The intellect, in its need to organise and measure, has also created the concept of space, the idea of a 'there' as well as 'here'. So we now have complex language and elaborate instruments for describing and measuring time and space. We view the universe as 'out there', an immense space which needs to be explored and understood. We send rockets into space to explore other planets. We speculate about the beginning of time in terms of the 'Big Bang' theory. We see ourselves as geographically and historically situated individuals, as separate persons thrown into a huge and impersonal world. The reality is that the world appears in us, at this very moment; it is unfolding to the awareness that we are… right here and right now. You may ask: why should mind have created time and space if they are not real? Why indeed! The important thing to recognise is that time and space are simply *concepts*; ideas formulated to explain experience. Even the concept of being a 'person' is just another false idea. In mistaking these concepts for reality, we have created a world-view that is based upon erroneous assumptions, and rarely do we question or challenge this orthodoxy. I hear you arguing: *"But I have to plan for tomorrow... there are things I need to do!"* Of course, these thoughts arise, and you may or may not act on them... but only ever in the present moment!

Let us keep it simple. Be fully present, and open up your awareness. Breathing is happening... seeing words is happening... thinking is happening. Whatever arises in consciousness is present right here and in this very moment. What we are aware of is here and now – this is all we ever have; all we can ever accept as real. Where else could we ever be except Here, and 'when' else could we be except Now?

The day's dreams ending
Night's dreams waiting
When will I wake up?

Death

One of the three marks of existence in Buddhism (*apart from 'suffering' and 'selflessness'*) is impermanence. Everything changes... nothing is permanent. Our common sense tells us this... whatever is born has to die. The old has to give way to the new. We know that our body cells are continuously dying in their millions, and that our whole bodies are totally renewed every seven years or so. Look at old photographs of yourself... that body no longer exists. Everything around us is changing, nothing is stable... there is nothing upon which to depend. We appear to be born, grow old, become sick, and then die. For most individuals those facts are profoundly troubling, and they seek security in beliefs about 'souls', and an eternally happy afterlife for those who behave themselves in this world.

If we believe that we are separate persons in the world, then of course the thought of not existing can be frightening and distressing. Individuals (*and their egos*) do not like to lose anything which diminishes their sense of identity, and death appears to be the ultimate loss. But again, let's keep it simple... actually *who* dies? If, as we have seen, we are not our bodies, and not our sensations, thoughts and feelings, then what is there to die? If what we truly are is pure awareness; that is outside of time and space; that was never born... how can that ever cease to be? Body and consciousness may arise and pass away... but what never changes? The still, shining and spacious awareness that is our true nature. Nothing personal remains... nothing of the illusory individual. Of course, trying to describe this real Self is impossible; because it has no qualities... it is no-thing. If we have never been separate from what is Real, then our apparent 'deaths' are no more significant than waves settling back into the ocean; water having always been their true nature. Our lives are no more important than movements (*whether they be mere ripples or storm-tossed waves*) on the surface of the ocean of Being. Patterns of energy moving through form and silence.

All that is True has its home in Silence. The truth in music lies in silence... in the space between notes. Without the absence of sound no music is possible (although John Cage may disagree!). The space between thoughts and sensations is the still emptiness of silence. It is the ground of Being, the Source, the Absolute. Here words fail, for it is No-Thing. IT is dimensionless; featureless; both absence and presence; emptiness and fullness. Only in silence can we know the Real. Discarding the unreal, we see what never changes. Whatever changes, arises and passes away – these are not real. All experiences, states of consciousness, perceptions, concepts... all are impermanent. The body and mind are constructs, and thus subject to change, suffering, and are not Self. Our true Self is not a thing; was not born, and thus cannot die.

Foxes mating...
New life starting
On the vegetable patch

Knowledge and Reality

How can we know anything? Conventional views of knowledge suggest that the mind generates understanding as a result of experience, and in turn these concepts and associated meanings are shared within language and culture. This intellectual knowing is founded upon words and conceptual thinking, and is therefore incapable of representing anything except personal interpretations. The word 'sugar' is not sweet; 'water' is not wet; and yet we understand what they mean. Words become pointers to the reality they represent. As discussed earlier, the mind loves to separate and label, and is essentially dualistic. The intellect objectifies lived experience, fossilising it within definitions. It enjoys the 'cut and thrust' of debate, seeking to rationalise and explain everything. Anything that defies rational explanation is viewed with the deepest suspicion, and dismissed as super-stition and religious belief. However, superstitions and religious beliefs are also the products of mental activity, and consist of concepts, albeit abstract and rarefied ones.

So, can we truly know anything? Within the limitations of language and conceptual thinking, probably not. The word is never the 'thing', and thoughts are just words. True knowing (*if we can call it that*) lies beyond the mind; beyond concepts. Whatever is described in non-duality prompts the mind to play the "*Yes, but...*" game. The ego (*which is merely the collection of memories we call 'me'*) is terrified by the idea of its non-existence, and will employ any intellectual argument to protect itself. True knowing has nothing to do with words or concepts... it is silent, choiceless awareness of what IS. It is not belief, not faith... it is a resting in *re-cognition* and *re-membrance*... upstream of thought, where emptiness is form, and form emptiness. What you truly are in this moment is cognising emptiness, it is actually 'non-being', from which all being-ness arises. You cannot know this in any fixed and finite way because it is infinite and ever fresh. All objects appear in this open space of knowing and nowhere else. All worlds appear in this infinite knowing... this singular Subjectivity includes everything objective. The bottom line is – "It's all a mystery!" – and that's why we need to be intellectually humble, and accept the limitations of our minds.

Our lives are collections of memories. Edited and incomplete memories at that. We carry them around as the luggage of our lives. So much baggage... often very heavy burdens. We top up these 'story bags', although they leak through holes in the bottom (as memories fade, disappear or become distorted). Our 'stories' are unique, dramatic, full of adventure, tragedies and joys. We take them to be real, and identify with them. We say: "I am my memories, thoughts, attitudes, ideas and opinions." We construct our selves and identities, and the habitual patterns of thinking and feeling become our 'personalities'. Then we get lost in the story of self. What a waste of energy!

Our first and last mistake is perceiving ourselves to be separate from one another. The purpose of our lives (if there is one) must be to re-member who we really are... to find that union... the Oneness that we lost as we grew up.

The rain on the window,
The dog snoring –
The Universe is all here.

Why do we take everything personally? All that appears to happen is perceived through the lens of 'I'... from the perspective of an illusory 'me'. All events are labelled and judged through a personal memory; and memory is simply the imperfect and edited recollection of appearances. Why do we depend on such fallible and finite recollections as a basis for life... our framework for living?

Mind as a thought-machine which solves practical problems, and for rational decision-making, is a wonderful tool. It can be utilised on the relative level to enable us to cope with everyday tasks and challenges. Where it 'oversteps the mark', however, is where belief systems are established to explain away mysteries and profound questions. The unanswerable is answered with a set of assumptions that create a doctrine or creed which simply closes the mind. All further exploration and investigation is abandoned. Answers are supplied for all of life's tricky questions, and the insecurity of 'not knowing' is banished. Even when answers are rejected, and seeking continues, this becomes a subtle form of identification. 'I' become a 'sceptic'; 'atheist'; 'agnostic'; a 'seeker'... the list goes on.

Can we drop all labels, all need to be 'someone'... and dwell in un-knowing awareness? Moving (apparently) through life and all it offers us in the form of sensations, thoughts and feelings... without accumulating the baggage of opinion, knowledge and belief? Is this possible?

What struggles we have! To become 'someone'... to achieve success, wealth, possessions, fame. Assuming that happiness and fulfilment are to be found in these things. How carefully we protect these trappings of ego... how frightened we are of losing these material possessions; but most of all, of losing ourselves... our identity. What a joke this turns out to be when we finally realise (if we do) that what we fear losing never truly existed. How much energy was wasted trying to protect and preserve a phantom!

Where there is desire…
There is movement.
Where there is movement…
There is agitation.
Where there is agitation…
There is conflict.
Where there is conflict…
There is no harmony.
Where there is no harmony…
There is no peace.
Where there is no peace…
There can be no love.
Where there is no love…
There is no Truth.

There is no separation. You are me... and I am you. The illusion of first and second person singular has gripped us from early childhood. What a tragedy... to divide us all into separate persons, leading separate lives, competing, comparing, confronting. What a delusory waste of time. Thought divides; but there are no thinkers. Thinking happens... just as walking, talking and sleeping happens. 'No one' is doing these things. Life is doing them. No one is being 'Graham' – Life is being 'Graham'; and when the energy that appears as this body-mind moves on to create another pattern, nothing has been lost or gained. As physics claims: energy cannot be created or destroyed... it simply changes form.

If we were responsible for thinking, if we are thinkers... wouldn't we choose our thoughts? Preferring pleasant happy thoughts to negative miserable ones? Watch a thought... where does it come from; what does it represent; and where does it go? We can only answer the second question, but that's with yet another thought. However, if we cease looking for answers in the mind, and turn our attention 180 degrees around to observe where thoughts appear (or what they appear in), there is only empty awareness – the Void which is capacity and space for all appearances/phenomena. 'It' isn't an object of thought; cannot be conceptualised, explained or defined. It is not any thing... it is what contains all things. It is what we truly are... we have just forgotten, overlooked and have been tricked into believing what we are not. It's not a matter of belief; just a matter of seeing. Of coming Home to where we always knew we belonged.

We can all do it now. Rest in that open spacious stillness (*words are so inadequate!*) that is your true identity. You are already and always there! Just wake up from your dream of living as a separate being, and become Everything. End the game of 'hide-and-seek' which you have been playing with yourself, and come out from the cupboard! Leave the darkness of ignorance and pretence, and be the Light of the world.

Simply being...
There is no becoming.
Simply observing...
There is no observer.
Watching...
No watcher.
Breathing...
No breather.
Experiencing...
No experiencer.
Why invent someone who doesn't exist?

Anyone who writes or speaks about this stuff must be crazy. No one wants to hear that they are no one! This news is desperately nihilistic. Quite hopeless. In fact hope is not what people need... it is hope that causes us to suffer. Hope offers us a better future; and the future does not exist. There is only this... here... now. And it doesn't get any better than this. This is as good as it gets. The mind doesn't want to hear that, as it lives in time, and hopes to continue into a better future. Simply being here, loving and accepting whatever arises, is the end of mind.

When we look closer, the mind doesn't actually exist. It consists of thoughts, feelings and memories, and none of these are real. The mind is a storyteller, a critic, and a nag; never giving us a moment's peace. The greatest story it creates is 'me'... the little self or ego. The story begins as soon as we feel separate from the world and others 'out there'... a separation which is encouraged from our earliest days as an infant. We are given a name, and told of 'things' that are 'not me'. We are indoctrinated to believe that we have a life to lead; and that we have the responsibility to make it a success. Success in this case means passing exams, getting a good career, making money, getting a partner, children, a house, a car... then a bigger house, a better car... and more and more stuff. And when we have all that? Are we happy? Perhaps, for a while. But often there's a feeling of emptiness; of futility; of something missing. In reality, nothing is missing; it's just that we have created an illusory prison called the 'story of me'; and we feel trapped inside it. Perhaps we can see through the story, realise there is no prison (there never was a prison), and be free?

The first lesson is: **we are not our body**. It would appear that we **have** a body, and therefore need to care **for** it... but we do not need to care **about** it, as it is not who we really are. Can you see the subtle difference? We can experience our body... see, feel and sense it in many ways; but these experiences come and go. The body changes, grows old, becomes ill, and dies. It is not under our control… it is not us. We are what experiences the body.

The second lesson is: **we are not the mind**. It seems as if we have a mind that consists of thoughts, feelings, ideas and concepts. These are constantly moving; a continuous stream of mental activity; rarely under our control. If the mind is only composed of these thoughts and emotions, and if they are incessantly changing, can the mind be said to truly exist? It is no more real than the images projected on to a cinema screen. The mind separates, classifies, judges; and creates the narrative of the self. It is a clever and absorbing tale, full of dramas; nevertheless it is fictional and ultimately unreal. This self, or ego, can be crafty and claim to be 'spiritually advanced', a seeker in search of enlightenment. The 'enlightened person' is an oxymoron… how can a mirage become anything? The ego creates the story of a life that needs to be meaningful and successful. We are usually lost in the drama… the dream of separation.

Waking up in the dream (or to the dream) means seeing (not knowing intellectually) that who we really are is not the body… and not the mind. What we are contains both body and mind… and everything else that can be perceived or conceived. What we are can never be described in words, cannot be defined or conceptualised. That would be the limited work of the mind. To become who we already are is the ambition of the spiritual seeker. How stupid! But what an enticing and entertaining game! We can spend a lifetime meditating, attending retreats, following gurus, balancing our *chakras*, and awakening our *kundalini*… for what? To reach liberation? To attain *nirvana*?

When we awake in the dream, there is a realisation that we are already whole; that we have never been anything but free. The mental prison that we created was just that… a fantasy that never existed. We were simply making our cell more comfortable, when the door was open all the time. There is nothing more to do. There might be more reading of books; mainly out of curiosity about how this message can be communicated in different ways. They are all Oneness talking to Oneness. If anyone ever reads these words, please remember: you are **not** who you think you are! You are Oneness trying to wake up... and perhaps these paltry words may help?

You were placed in a prison as a child... a prison made of words and ideas. The idea of name, sex, personality, race, religion, values, morals, attitudes and so on. All these were indoctrinated and conditioned into a false self... The individual you think you are today. Wake up! Wake up to the dream and be who you are, beyond any concept or even any experience. Or wait until death, when you will wake up **from** the dream.

Why do all people think they decide what happens in their lives?

Is it the illusion of control… and free will?

If everything is a part of God… and God is in all things…

then whatever happens to us is the Divine expressing itself through us.

There is no separate little self which manages its destiny,

and the assumption that it can shape its own future

is the supreme arrogance of the ego.

Do you think consciousness resides in the brain?

Would you take your television set apart in search of the actors in your favourite soap opera?

Would you search the cinema screen for the images that appear upon it?

Would you come to understand a tree through studying a single leaf?

There is nothing... absolutely nothing... that mind can create that is permanent. All is like the mist in the morning sunshine... it evaporates completely. Thoughts, perceptions, feelings, memories... all drift through consciousness like clouds across the sky... coming into view and then disappearing... leaving no trace. The grasping after these thoughts and sensations leads to memories and desires. If thoughts are chased and held they create traces, and delusions come into being. We collect these traces to manufacture our egos or sense of identity... producing an illusion of permanence and of separate being.

There is consciousness of awareness, acting as the canvas on which all life is painted (or screen on which all experience – the 'show' – is projected)... and even consciousness is transient. What is eternal and infinite is awareness... our true identity.

There is a moment, not caught up in the movement of time
   … when the breath holds on to the present,
   … the whirlwind of the mind ceases to spin,
   … and the world becomes still.
   As the muddy water settles in the pond… so the lotus flower emerges
   … purity from filth.
   Greens so green that the word becomes meaningless…
   Blues so blue that the sky laughs for joy!

   Beneath the clatter and chatter of thought…
   Beyond the good and the bad; yes and no; up and down;
   The 'higher third' awaits…
   Ready to greet the silence with a secret smile.

Imagine you are wearing glasses – special glasses that have the world and all its happenings appearing on the inside of the each lens, like a cinema screen. Every image, sensation, thought and feeling can be experienced by wearing these magic glasses. We are captivated by the spectacle (pardon the pun!). These scenes are actually experienced; so moving, talking and thinking happens in them. This is our world as we live it, and we assume it is real and all there is.

Now what if we remove these glasses? The images, concepts and experiences disappear. What remains is what was always there – the shining empty stillness that contains everything. It has no name because it is not a concept... not a thing. All the time attention was focussed on the inside of the glasses (*entrancing though the show was*), what was real was not seen. No special practices are needed to allow the clear seeing of what is Real; no beliefs or teachers or books; just removal of what was unreal. What is now seen cannot be understood or described... it is outside all previous experience. It has no reference point... no dimensions... It never changes.

Life is like a huge game of Hide-and-Seek. God is playing this game with Herself... continuously inventing new ways of pretending to be 'other'. New appearances... new stories... new dramas... all apparently convincing. So convincing, indeed, that she forgets (or pretends to forget) who she really is, and indulges in a fantasy of being separate. Seven billion fantasies, in fact, all being played out simultaneously, with consummate skill. The most wonderful 'soap opera'. The plot and the script are being written spontaneously, with no ulterior motive or purpose other than the sheer joy of creation. No hidden agenda... no rules to follow... no prizes to win. This game is wonderful fun for God, who would be dreadfully bored if there were no separate 'characters' to invent and play with. She knows, of course, that in actuality there are no 'things' apart from Herself, but the 'make-believe' is simply patterns of energy within one field... interdependent and mutually arising. Like waves on the surface of the ocean... all appearing to be separate but made of the same substance, and always settling back to become part of that from which they came.

What fun...
This emptiness –
So full of stuff!

A Dialogue

One day (*but of course in truth there are no 'days'*) God thought it would be fun to play this game with one of her 'characters'… to find out whether the 'person' could see through the game and laugh at the absurdity of feeling separate. So what follows is a dialogue between this person and a 'sage' (one of those apparent characters who have seen the game for what it is, and are no longer fooled by its appearances).

Person: Who am I?

Sage: Why do you ask?

P: Because I once thought I knew who I was… but when I start to look closer and try to find some permanent or separate individual… it's elusive… almost impossible.

S: Good… keep looking closer… inwards. Searching externally for an identity is easy… you can always find labels and descriptions, ranging from gender, nationality, religion, politics, occupation, through to all the baggage of opinions, beliefs and memories that we carry around.

P: Yes… I checked my CV recently, and it's rather meaningless; just a collection of labels and stories – not me in any real sense. Is there anything unique or special about me?

S: Only in the way that Life has been expressed (is expressing) Itself through sensing, thinking and feeling. Those reflections of awareness are perhaps unique… **but** the light of that awareness is infinite, non-dual, noumenal, containing and reflecting all.

P: So I don't really exist?

S: Not the individual you think you are. In reality, you are everything and nothing.

P: So should I stop searching for who I am?

S: There may be more searching… maybe not. It is simpler to stay with the awareness of being… not saying "I am this" or "I am that". Just "I am". Allow that sense to grow to encompass all.

Any description or label you apply to yourself is inevitably unreal and limited – who you **really** are is more than the mind can accommodate. Who you really, **really** are is the most wonderful secret and surprise – beyond words and imagination... and you have always been and always will be That (*even though time does not exist*). You cannot move away from That... it is your true identity.

P: So I should just 'be'... and stop looking?

S: You cannot not 'be'... you are the Source of all; the ground of the Real.

P: ... But who I think I am... this person – is that all illusion?

S: Yes. An elaborate story devised by the mind. It remains as long as the mind preserves and protects this separate selfhood, but will dissolve when it is seen as the mirage it is in reality.

P: Why is this sense of being an individual created? It seems such a stupid and cruel trick!

S: The answer to that lies beyond the mind. The nature of the mind is to conceptualise... to create ideas, systems and beliefs. The mind will only develop another conceptual framework to explain why it does what it does... it cannot get 'behind' or 'upstream' of itself. Perhaps we can think of Life (or God) playing a game of 'hide-and-seek' with Itself... and eventually all the players will win.

P: So how to play this game?

S: There's no 'how'... the game is playing itself. The drama is unfolding spontaneously within the consciousness that is witnessing it. There is only awareness, and the contents of that awareness.

P: Why am I here?

S: Well, let's deal with these words and what they may mean. We have stated that the "I" you think you are doesn't exist in reality. It is the creation of the mind; which also has created the concepts of time and space, so the word "here" is also meaningless.

P: We are talking right now… right here?

S: Yes – talking is happening, and in this moment there is freedom from time and space. It is the mind which needs to measure and locate everything. All there is, is **this**. Just this… leave everything else alone. Before your next thought… stop! In that silent space is all you need.

P: So is there a purpose to my life?

S: Is there any purpose to the waves on the ocean? Their appearance and disappearance do not change or affect the ocean in the slightest. On a more relative level, you may say that your life is an opportunity for Life to find itself.

P: What's the point of that?

S: That's the mystery! The play of the Universe (*Lila*) is an apparent game played for its own sake. All things apparently arising and passing away… coming into seeming existence from the fullness of the Void, and returning to it. Causelessly, without meaning or purpose. Any meaning that is put on the process by the mind is simply a limited interpretation… not Truth… which lies far beyond words and mind.

P: So we cannot find the answers in the mind?

S: The mind will provide many answers, and create elaborate theories and belief systems to seek to explain the mystery of Life. Most people settle for these apparent answers, and stop asking the important questions: "Who am I?" and "Why am I here?"

P: But if there are no understandable answers to these questions, why ask them?

S: Because the asking allows us to move beyond the mind… refusing to accept the intellect's answers keeps us open to the Truth that is within… always available to us… so close that it is impossible to move towards it… it is who/what we really are. Realising this, all questions fall away.

P: So is the secret to keep asking the questions, without expecting any answers?

S: Stay with the questions, yes… and allow understanding to

arise from simply Being. Don't look outside yourself for answers or guidance. All answers are waiting in silence within. Look inside… keeping what you know is certain in front of you.

P: I'm not sure I know anything for certain!

S: You know that you **are**, don't you? There is the certainty of existing; of simply being alive?

P: Yes, I know I **am**… but not what or why!

S: Never mind the what or why – just focus on the sense of 'being'; the 'I am' – and stay with that. There is a vast silence, emptiness and stillness in simply being – you need nothing more than to rest there – everything else is already there, waiting to be recognised as who, what and why you truly are.

P: OK… so I know 'I am', and I also understand that any labels or concepts that I use to explain my 'purpose' are the result of thought, and therefore limited.

S: Of course, so just rest in the awareness of being.

P: … and so how do I live my life?

S: You don't… Life is living you!

P: So I just sit back and allow things to happen?

S: Things happen spontaneously anyway; why put effort into pretending that you are exerting any control over them?

P: So things just happen… with no reason, cause or purpose?

S: Things happen just the way they are supposed to happen… perfectly and causelessly.

P: So all the children in Africa dying from AIDS is a perfect happening?

S: Those things are apparently happening, but it is our minds that label them good or bad.

P: So an innocent child dying unnecessarily is neither good nor bad?

S: Exactly… and who says it is unnecessary? Everything seems to happen because it has to.

P: What do you mean "seems to happen"?

S: Our perception of 'things happening' is only the interpretation by the mind of sensory input, isn't it? A result of labelling, conceptualising and putting these memories together to produce a story. We build these stories about 'ourselves' and the 'world' to create a sense of continuity and purpose. This relative level of functioning is what we assume to be reality… but it's only the game of life which we take so seriously.

P: So life is just a game?

S: Yes – a wonderful magic show, with no real substance – a mind-created entertainment.

P: So it doesn't matter how we behave? We can go out and rob and murder others, and it won't matter?

S: The 'person' we appear to be will act according to its conditioning. If you have been programmed by your culture and experience not to rob and murder, 'you' are highly unlikely to start now.

P: So I have no control over my life?

S: So long as you continue to think of 'you' living 'your life', you will be missing the point. Who is there to 'live your life'? If you cannot find an individual 'you', then there cannot be anyone to exercise free will.

P: So life is just happening… with no purpose at all?

S: Life is happening spontaneously, yes… and who is there to understand any purpose? It is only the mind that seeks reasons and meaning… and the mind can never comprehend something that is larger than itself, that contains all there is… and yet holds nothing.

P: This all sounds so ridiculous… I don't know what to think about anything any more… my head's spinning!

S: That's a good sign… let it spin… and shake all the beliefs out. Belief is not needed… just direct knowing.

P: I thought all knowledge comes from the mind?

S: This type of knowing does not need the mind; it is before thought… prior to any mental activity… it is a direct and immediate seeing. When you awake from a dream you see directly and immediately that it was not real. If you have dreamt that your house was on fire... do you phone the fire brigade when you wake up?

P: No, of course not. So I need to stop thinking... to still the mind... through meditation? Is that the answer?

S: You can't stop the mind thinking... that is what it does... what it is designed for. And meditation is not about quietening the mind... it is letting go of the stream of thought... just stepping back to observe. Even that description is misleading in its dualism; there is no-one and no-thing to observe in reality.

P: So words are useless to describe what we are talking about?

S: Yes... the word is never the thing... and we are not talking about any 'thing' anyway! Words can act as signposts pointing in the right direction, but in reality there is no place to go other than right here; and no time to be other than right now. What we seek we already are... we are already home, but we simply don't recognise it... we have forgotten it.

P: I just don't get it!

S: Of course not – the mind will never 'get it'! The mind can only label and differentiate, creating 'things' and dividing into separate parts what is in reality one Whole. The mind has also created the 'ego', this sense of a separate self... and will do all it can to preserve and protect its creation. The ego is constantly fighting against its greatest fear – that of not existing. It will do everything it can to maintain a sense of identity... of being a 'subject' in a world of 'objects'.

P: So should I try to still the mind?

S: You can try... but the 'trying' is still the activity of the mind... like a puppy trying to catch its own tail.

P: This is crazy... it's impossible!

S: Yes – it's all impossibly, delightfully mad. Trying to understand at an intellectual level is also impossible... like the eye trying to see itself.

P: So I should give up trying?

S: Then 'giving up' becomes another type of mental activity… a subtler form of seeking.

P: Aaaargh!

S: Yes! Stay with that… go into it. Just watch the frustration of the intellect… the next question arising… the mind's: "Yes… but"! The self has to justify its existence through inquiry and explanations. That's why belief systems are so popular.

P: What's wrong with belief?

S: Belief involves the unreal; supporting what is not the case; and ignoring what **is**. It creates illusion and delusion… and does not help one to distinguish what is true from what is untrue. Belief has nothing to do with Truth. Truth is closer to you than your own breath… it is your birthright; your very nature… where is there a need for belief? Why believe anything, when you can know, with great certainty, what is Real?

P: To know something requires learning?

S: Not necessarily. We learn many things through experience, through being taught, and through teaching ourselves; but there is a form of knowledge that does not depend on words, or any form of transmission. It is a form of direct seeing… wordless, without concepts, ideas or mental activity of any kind. It is the knowing… or recognition… that does not need or involve the mind. You know, without any shadow of doubt, that you exist, don't you?

P: Well, yes… I suppose so.

S: No suppose about it… you are! Here and now… you exist… right?

P: Yes… I accept that I am aware right now. But isn't that just my brain activity?

S: There is a material response to this 'awareness' in your brain, yes. It can be demonstrated through EEG, etc. But let's keep this simple… the brain is just another concept. Conscious awareness – the sense of being present – that is beyond the brain, upstream of the mind. The mind and its thoughts, feelings and sensations… all appear within this awareness. This awareness is outside space and time, and therefore infinite and eternal.

P: Is that who I really am?

S: Yes… but the sense of a personal 'you' is an illusion to be seen through. Letting go of this little self allows the possibility of the real Self to emerge. That is who 'you' **really** are… that emptiness/fullness. Nothing left out – never born – and so will never die… nothing 'personal' at all.

P: So I've never made a decision in my life?

S: It appeared as if 'you' did… but in reality there is no one there to decide anything. Events just unfolded within consciousness… ever here and now… causelessly and without purpose.

P: Do you mean… meaninglessly?

S: What meaning or purpose do you want? Isn't it the mind that seeks meaning and rationale – in order to bolster the false sense of ego?

P: But I remember deciding to have toast for breakfast instead of porridge!

S: The memory of what apparently happened is appearing now in your awareness… one of a succession of thoughts.

P: So my memory is false?

S: Memory is just thought appearing now.

P: So I didn't have toast for breakfast?

S: Of course… on our level of reality (which may be no more than a dream) you have a present memory of what seemed to happen. But on the 'absolute' level of non-duality – nothing happened – or ever happened. For 'things' to happen, duality is required. There is a need for a subject and an object… time and space. All these are concepts – products of the mind.

P: So everything is unreal?

S: All conceptual phenomena, including time and space, have no ultimate reality. However, in the relative world in which we appear to live, things seem to exist, and events happen by themselves.

P: By themselves? Without cause or purpose?

S: There may be conditions and causes which appear to produce results, but essentially Life appears spontaneously… just the way it is… without meaning.

P: So life has no meaning?

S: Meaning is created by the mind… and our minds are part of the appearance, so how could a mind possibly comprehend what contains it?

P: What contains the mind then?

S: Awareness… consciousness itself, which is the background to all phenomena. The screen on which the mind, body and senses project the world. That which is our true nature… our Being.

P: So the world appears in awareness?

S: Yes… everything appears in the conscious awareness that we really and truly are.

P: I used to think that I appeared in the world… but it's actually the other way round?!

S: Absolutely – who you really are is the creator and destroyer of worlds. Without awareness no 'thing' could exist. But awareness itself does not exist apart… this would imply being within time and space, and becoming an object which is experienced by a subject. No, this awareness is the ultimate Subject, without any object… not in time and space… limitless, birthless, deathless – eternal. It cannot be known, described, perceived or 'objectified' in any way. Because it is beyond knowing, the brain/mind will never 'get it'… it cannot be understood in phenomenal terms. It is noumenal. There is understanding which has nothing to do with knowledge… but the mind must fall silent for it to arise. Such understanding cannot be taken, but it may be granted… there may be 'Grace'.

P: You make it sound very mystical.

S: Only because the mind cannot grasp this intellectually. As I said, the intellect must be put aside for understanding to arise. In actuality, there is nothing mystical or mysterious about this... it is so simple and so close that we have simply overlooked what is... This... just This. We have been looking in the wrong places... outside ourselves... whilst all the time Truth has been here... within.

P: So we can look for Truth?

S: Not as an intellectual search... that will be fruitless. But simply asking, "Who am I?" will help to discover the silent stillness and spaciousness that is always available. You will find there is no one to find Truth... no one to become enlightened.

P: So no one decides to do anything?

S: Actions happen... no one does them.

P: So I should just sit back and do nothing?

S: We have been here before! Just remember – at an absolute level, there is no 'you' to either sit back or to rush into activity. On a relative level, however, it appears as if things happen because of mind-body activity. These happenings result from conditions... an intricate range of influencing factors... all pre-determined.

P: So there's no free will or choice in any action or behaviour?

S: Choice would require a 'chooser', and in reality there is none.

P: So things just happen?

S: Why shouldn't they? Things happen... or rather, appear to happen... as happening involves time and space, both of which are dualistic concepts. These apparent events may seem random, but may in fact be the perfect expression of Reality... just the appearance that is necessary... here and now.

P: So I should simply sit back and watch the show?

S: In a way, yes... but really there is no one to watch the show... you **are** the show!

P: I am the show?

S: What you truly are is an expression of Reality... Life having fun; pretending to be a 'self' searching for Itself. Whatever you perceive, think or sense that you are is only an aspect of Oneness... you cannot be anything else. There is no little 'me' looking out on to the world; the world appears in you... you are the world; the timeless reality... the Non-dual.

P: So my doubts, fears, insecurities are all part of Oneness... of God?

S: Of course. You may not feel very 'divine' when worrying about your life; or being depressed and anxious... but in essence you cannot be anything but God. It's just that you've forgotten who you really are, and have identified with your body and mind. Recognise what you truly are by looking... not by more thinking... not by conceptualising and objectifying Reality. It is not a thing... not a state... not an experience. It is not in time or space, so is not 'out there' or 'in here'... nor can it be achieved tomorrow or at some future point. It is here... now. It is the sound of the wind outside, the ticking of the clock, the sense of weight on the chair, the light coming in the window... just This!

P: It can't be **just** this!

S: The mind is saying that. It's the mind that wants spiritual fireworks, the pinnacle of enlightenment after strenuous practise; the success of attainment. It's all ego stuff; very subtle egoism perhaps, but still the maintenance of a separate self who can be 'special'. It's still in the trap of dualism.

Listen, it's so simple – there is **only** the Self... **only** Oneness. All arises within the Oneness – thoughts, feelings, sensations – and we assume they are real. They are no more real than a dream. They are the dream we call living; but it is a mirage... images projected on to the screen of awareness. The screen itself remains untouched by whatever image it reflects... joys, sadnesses, triumphs and tragedies. All are essentially unreal. We create the world by such experiences, and yet fail to realise that all experiences are transient and illusory.

The story of our 'selves' is also manufactured by the mind,

which is a machine producing dualistic concepts. It labels and judges 'things', perceives them as separate objects (from the reference point of an imagined self), and this creates the story of 'me' and the 'world'. Pure awareness does not distinguish between self and other, between subject and object. It is beyond the mind; 'upstream' of thought. Where conceptual thinking divides, awareness unites. No concepts – no self – no problem!

P: You make it sound so easy.

S: What's hard about it? It's only the mind trying to understand it that creates the difficulty... but realise that the mind will **never** understand this... will never 'get it'. It's like the hand trying to hold itself... the teeth attempting to bite themselves... the fish searching for water. Once the impossibility is seen, there is a letting go... an acceptance... a resting in Silence. Then the Real can be... as if the clouds have left the sky clear and blue – and the light of Truth shines unhindered... as it always has done and always will... timelessly.

P: So I have to let go of everything?

S: Be careful here... even the 'letting go of everything' is an action of intent... a subtle movement of the ego. There is no one to let go of anything. All motive must be dropped. Any movement, in any direction, is a movement away from This... Here... Now. Nothing needs to be done... everything is perfect just as it is.

P: What?! Even the killing, pain and suffering across the world?

S: All appearances in the dream... it is the mind that judges 'things' as good or bad. Whereas, everything is appropriate.

P: So we should accept everything as OK?

S: You will accept or not according to your conditioned mind. But in reality, there are no mistakes.

P: So Hitler and Stalin were perfect?

S: Both were 'appearances' in the dream we call life. We attach judgments to these apparent persons and bring them to 'life'...

but they are fictional characters, as we all are.

P: Then what is real?

S: Nothing you can name or describe. All such labelling is merely 'mind-stuff'.

P: So what am I to do?

S: Examine this closely... and ask yourself: "Who is there to act? To whom do these questions arise? Who or what am I?"

P: The practice of *vichara* – self-inquiry.

S: Yes... but don't answer the questions. Let them echo in the silence of your true nature. Any answers which come from your mind are incorrect. Just pursue the questions... "Who is asking the questions? Who is wanting answers?"

SILENCE

P: There is a seeing that everything is empty and no-thing exists.

S: Yes... anything that is experienced – physically, mentally, spiritually – is unreal.

P: So if all this is unreal... what matters?

S: In the absolute sense... nothing matters.

P: So there is no point in doing anything?

S: Such as...?

P: Well – spiritual practice?

S: Who is there to practise?

P: Well, me of course... but then you tell me there is no 'me'!

S: I don't tell you anything... but ask you to look for yourself.

P: Look here... there's no me... and everything is utterly pointless. So why don't I just give up and do nothing?

S: Your question is based on a false premise – that there is someone to either act or not. There's no 'you' to do anything... but the conditioned mind will continue to function. There are actions but no 'actor'.

P: So I'm not responsible for my actions?

S: Who is there to be responsible?

P: The same old response! How tedious!!

S: OK... let's look at this another way. There are thoughts, feelings, actions... yes?

P: Of course.

S: They arise and pass away?

P: Yes... all the time.

S: Do you control them?

P: Sometimes I do.

S: When? Give me an example.

P: Well – I might choose to go for a walk.

S: In the dream one makes choices... or so it appears. A thought might arrive: "A walk would be good." Action may follow – but on an absolute level there is thinking, but no thinker... acting, but no actor.

P: So we are puppets! With no control over our lives?

S: Everything arises in awareness... including apparent people leading apparent lives. The present awareness is what we truly are – not what comes and goes on the screen of consciousness. Confusion as well as understanding both arise and pass away – ultimately they are unimportant.

P: So liberation is unimportant? Not to be sought?

S: Liberation is just another concept... to keep the seeker busy seeking. If understanding and insight arise – they arise for no one. Without so-called 'awakening' life continues to be seen as real – attachments and aversions will occur, and suffering will continue if there is identification with the body and mind.

P: So we should not identify with the body or mind?

S: Listen to your own question. The word "should" implies a right or wrong way to live. Life unfolds just the way it needs to... judgments of good or bad are merely of the mind. Without thought there is no 'right' or 'wrong'. If we become attached to our thoughts, feelings or sensations, 'we' become lost in the dream, mistaking the illusion for reality. Waking in the dream is simply seeing what is unreal and what is real.

A Break from Dialogue

What is being written simply appears on the computer screen. Writing is happening but there is no writer. There is an appearance of choice, but Life is unfolding just as it is... in this everlasting Now. Plans for tomorrow, next month, next year appear in thought, become attached with desires, fears and the little self. They stick like goosegrass... little hooks enmeshing more thoughts and emotions, loading the mind, burdening consciousness. Consciousness is naturally spacious and clear, but the screen of awareness can so soon become full of 'mind-stuff'. It's all unreal, of course, and makes no impact or mark on the screen whose nature is Emptiness. It is Emptiness that draws us... Oblivion that we seek... but in seeking something else or 'other' we miss the open secret: that Emptiness just means **letting go**. Letting go of the little separate self with all its imagined troubles and plans. Seeing through the illusion of separateness, and relaxing into the embrace of empty Fullness... our true home.

Normally the mind will be asking, "How to let go?" Will be wanting more answers and explanations. More books, more teachers, more satsangs and retreats... one more push and we'll get there! Where? We look in the wrong direction... outside of us. If we turn round 180 degrees and look within, there'll be nowhere to go, and nothing to do... because there's no one to do it! There is just this... perfect – just how it should be – beyond thought, beyond self. And so the show goes on (or so it seems) – appearances arise within awareness... incessantly unfolding a world in the Now.

Church bells, birdsong, bees humming, dogs barking... hearing is happening.

Tea and toast... tasting is happening.

Roses and chocolate cake... smelling is happening.

The squiggles on the screen... seeing is happening.

The warmth of the sun... the softness of the cushion in my back... sensing and touching are happening.

Thoughts, ideas, words and associated emotions are arising... mental activity is happening.

Everything happening Now... to no one. Everything arising Now... in the stillness and infinite space of Awareness.

Just this aliveness; this Being.

Just this Joy and Love unfolding playfully; purposelessly, with no agenda or aim, except to express Life.

Before thought... before labelling and judging... before all the activity of the little 'me'... there's just This.

A Brief Chat

P: So how do I realise that?

S: **You** don't… 'you' can't realise anything!

P: It's all hopeless then?

S: Yes… this is a message of hopelessness, helplessness and despair… you might as well just give up; let go… and find peace… or rather Peace will become what you are.

P: So I can choose to do anything…

S: **You** can't choose… Life is living you. There's no 'you' to choose anything.

P: So anything goes? I can go out and mug some old lady for her money?

S: You might… but with your apparent preferences and programming it seems unlikely. Either way, it is an apparent drama unfolding in the story of 'your' life… and you may regard it as important, and hold the delusion that you decided to act in a certain way.

P: So there are preferences which are personal?

S: It would seem that the mind-body organism that appears here has certain mental habits and the 'circuitry' is conditioned to act in a predictable fashion. But… there is no one 'pulling the strings' – no thinker – just thinking; no actor – just acting; no person – Life having fun, creating an apparent life-story. There are infinite ways in which Life can seek itself… pretending to hide from itself in the most basic or grotesque forms… but laughing at its own ingenuity and creativity. Death of apparent individuals results in Life being reunited with its invention… liberation or 'enlightenment' means this can happen before death. However, the word "before" implies time… and there isn't any! So-called 'enlightenment' means the death of the person… so no one can become 'enlightened'.

P: Why is this message not understood or available more

widely?

S: Because it's dangerous and subversive. What could be more threatening to individuals than to be told that they do not exist... that they are illusions? It is the most unacceptable message for the ego/mind which will do all it can to preserve the pretence of a separate existence.

P: What do you mean by "pretence"?

S: Well, think of it like a game that Life (God... Brahman... whatever) is playing with Itself. The nearest analogy is the game of hide-and-seek. Life seeks some entertainment through pretending to hide from itself in the form of persons. These people have forgotten who they really are (the game being played so well) so that Life has great fun in hiding from itself very convincingly, and only manages to reveal itself to itself in (apparently) a small minority of the population. However, everyone will be found eventually, and the game will be over. It seems, though, that Life is enjoying the game so much that it doesn't want it to finish; and is hiding from itself in increasingly complex and inscrutable ways.

P: It sounds like a particularly cruel game to me!

S: It might appear that way... with all the human suffering that seems evident; but remember that in reality there are no persons; this is one enormous hoax. If we believe we exist as separate beings in an alien and hostile world, then that's the game being played with brilliant ingenuity. Don't forget that the game analogy is just that... a way of pointing towards the inexpressible. There is **no one** to become enlightened, but Life may lift the clouds of self-ignorance in places, to reveal the light of Self-knowledge to itself. There is only Life and its appearances – nothing outside – no one to be lost.

P: Are there questions that can act as signposts or guides towards this self-recognition?

S: Oh yes... many good questions! The finest is "Who am I?" Asking, "Why?" invites the mind to become active in inventing answers… and any answer that comes from the mind is limited, constrained by memory, and crippled by language and concepts. Asking, "Who am I?" leads the mind to look inside, not outside to the world. Looking within leads the mind to silence, as answer after answer are dismissed… the *via negativa* (*Neti… Neti*: not this… not this). Allow the mind to become still… simply BE… and truth can emerge and be recognised; wordlessly and non-conceptually. Truth is recognised deep within the heart… the intellect is redundant. Once seen, all that's left to us is to have a good laugh… or at least a smile!

We are God.
We have forgotten this.
The purpose of life is to remember this.
As babies we knew this,
But personal stories got in the way.
We think we are in the world
But the world is in us.
Everything and Nothing is what we truly are.

Floating

Imagine that you are floating in the middle of a huge ocean. Wherever you look there is no sign of land. Sometimes the waves are small and merely nudge you this way and that. Sometimes the waves are bigger and throw you around violently.

This is the ocean of Life... sometimes smooth and calm; at other times rough and stormy.

Occasionally you see pieces of driftwood floating by. Some are large and you climb on top; others are small and all you can do is to hold on with your hands. Fear of drowning forces you to grasp on to the nearest piece of wood that comes your way. Perhaps after a while you see another piece which looks stronger and more supportive, and so you swim to that and cling on as hard as you can. Your raft gives you a sense of security and hope.

You are not alone in this ocean. Most people that you meet are clinging to driftwood. Some join you on yours; others are grasping other pieces of wood. You, and the others holding on to your wood, convince each other that they have chosen the strongest and most dependable raft. Other rafts, you believe, are doomed to sink and their occupants will drown. Just as long as you hold on tightly, you will be saved.

One day, you spot someone who is not holding on to any wood, but just floating on the surface of the water. You call over and invite him to join you on your raft. He smiles and replies: "No thanks... there's no need for a raft. If you can simply let go, the ocean will support you. Everything is taken care of, and there's no need to fear anything." He continued: "Your rafts are your belief systems... you believe they will save you from the ocean; but that's impossible. You are surrounded by the ocean, moving with it, supported by it. Why resist? Why fight it? Why fear it? Let go! Everything will be all right... you are safe."

Very few people let go of their rafts of belief (be they

Christian, Muslim, Buddhist, Hindu, Socialist, Atheist, etc.). The few who do will discover that they were always supported by the ocean of Life… that they did not need to resist or fear it; and it's far more enjoyable to lay back and float!

Happiness is not pleasure
Happiness brings freedom
Pleasure brings bondage

The world appears in awareness... all that is experienced is a construction of the mind. Included in that is the sense of a personal self... it is a fond fiction responsible for most of the suffering that appears to happen... a drama within a dream.

How liberating... to be nothing but a dream! Nothing real happens within a dream – it is all imagination; the production of an overactive mind. How tiring to be caught up with such silliness... assuming the charade to be real. Everything is an expression of Oneness, agreed, but what an unhelpful and tiresome expression it can be! Waking up in the dream enables a 'seeing through' of this mirage; a letting go of old illusions. No separation... no self... no problem!

The dream keeps us (apparently) separated... separate from each other and our True Self. The dream consists of false beliefs and assumptions; namely, that we are the body, the mind, and a sense of 'persona' or personal self. Wake up! Just look... if you lost both your arms and both legs, would you still be you? Even with a heart, liver and lung transplant, would you still exist? Of course! Consciousness would still be present – thoughts, feelings and sensations would still arise. Do you imagine that consciousness arises in the head? Is the seat of being in the brain? Or is the infinite energy that is Life simply using the speck of consciousness called 'you' to express itself? Can it be that our neurones are simply transmitting waves of energy to manifest as individual points of consciousness?

In a relative sense, of course, individuals exist for a while, but not independently from everything else. Is a wave independent of the ocean? Of course not... it arises from the ocean, and falls back into the ocean. It always was, and always will be, the ocean.

Our minds, which are only temporary and limited collections of thoughts and emotions, convince themselves that they are separate and important. They create the ego, the lonely self who senses that it has to struggle to survive in an alien and hostile world. The egoic mind has been corrupted and programmed from an early age to regard itself as a little self who needs an identity. This conditioning creates a fictional individual with a name, gender, ethnicity, and a host of opinions. These labels construct a 'person' who feels not only separated from others, but also obliged to protect a self-concept and self-esteem which is totally fictional. What a tragic joke!

All that we seem to be is actually energy moving through form. That is all that every 'thing' is; including apparent people. Energy is not divided, cannot be created, and cannot be destroyed. Every apparent 'thing' is simply an expression of Energy (call it Life, Love, Absolute, God, etc.) and we/you are That. We/you were therefore never born and will never die. Can you see?

If we live for 80 years, there are about 4,000 weeks in which to discover who or what we are, and what we are doing here. The first 1,000 weeks are spent becoming programmed and conditioned by our parents, friends and culture. We are taught to be acquisitive; to become 'someone'; to accumulate stuff; and to develop our self-image or ego. We get so lost in this 'me' story that most spend our remaining 3,000 weeks lost in this tale of delusion and suffering. Some may ask deeper questions about life after 2,000 weeks or so (around the age of 40… when we start to reflect and take stock of our lives). We may have accumulated stuff as we were instructed: spouse, children, career, house, car, etc. Then we perhaps stop and ask: "Is this all there is?" "Is this all that life means?"

Many find answers to their questions in the form of religious belief systems. These provide stock answers which may satisfy some, and offer the reward of 'eternal life' if beliefs are accepted and followed. Very few continue to search. Some will identify with the Absolute, Brahman, Buddha, Christ, etc… and adopt a spiritual identity, but a subtle sense of ego remains… the 'awakened' person or 'advanced soul'. If all 'personas' are seen through and dropped, what remains? Simply Life; appearing as energy; expressing itself through forms... material, mental and 'spiritual'.

The 'bottom line' is this: nothing matters! Why? Because Nothing IS!

Nothing ever happened, is happening, or will ever happen.

All 'this' is energy moving through form... that's all.

There's nothing personal in anything that appears... it's a magic show.

Whether the show is accompanied by feelings of fear, depression, anxiety or happiness makes absolutely no difference.

It's all a mirage.

So drop all identification with a separate entity, a personal story... that's simply diverting energy into useless paths.

Even if identification continues, and 'suffering' appears to happen... that's still just energy moving.

Nothing's wasted or gained.

This is as good as it gets, so...

Feast on life... stop 'shopping'!

Beyond description and explanation. This cannot be known or comprehended... cannot be understood or experienced. Knowledge and experience belong to the mind, which functions in time and space.

Beyond knowledge and experience – beyond time and space – nothing and everything exists.

This cannot be found and cannot be avoided... there is no movement towards or away from This. It embraces all... sensations; thoughts; feelings... all are manifesting This... there is only ONE.

The wind that moves the grass... the sun that warms the skin... the hands that type these words... the words appearing on the screen... all are expressions of Life.

Life is enjoying its own expressions... the divine playful game of 'Lila'… God's entertainment.

Not just the perfection of clouds in a blue sky… or a young rose; but also the bodies of dead slugs… the decaying old rose… the dog excrement… all this… everything… is God. The joy, hope, satisfaction, worry, agitation, fear and despair… all… all is God/Life/One.

Let me state a few things that appear to be self-evident:

I am not a person… or any 'thing'.

I perceive the body and the mind; therefore I cannot be what I perceive.

The body-mind appears in awareness.

Whatever appears in awareness changes.

Whatever changes cannot be real or true.

A person is a constant stream of changing sensations, thoughts and images… and therefore a 'person' cannot be real.

I am… but am not what arises and passes in awareness.

I am… but not in time or space, which are mental constructs.

Awareness (which I am) is Here and Now; outside of time and space.

Therefore what I am was never born and can never die.

There are no things… only processes… appearances in awareness.

Phenomena are just patterns of energy transforming themselves. Think of the space within this room… it contains and allows all things to exist within it… without resistance. Tables, chairs, objects, bodies… even non-material things like thoughts and emotions are all manifestations of energy. So-called 'material' objects are mainly space and not matter, as quantum physics has revealed. Everything is changing, transforming energy which cannot be created or destroyed, but is simply taking on new forms.

The mind 'reifies' – constructs, creates, classifies, criticises… it's very good at what it does… it is 'minding'. Mental activity as electrical energy can be shown on EEGs and fMRI scans, but it doesn't matter if this activity takes place in the amygdala, prefrontal cortex and or anywhere in the brain... the fact is that any mental activity is simply a form of energy appearing in awareness. Nothing special; and nothing to waste too much time in investigating. As if we could pinpoint our 'self' through tracking down electrical impulses! What foolishness!

The story of a person appears in awareness – a plausible hologram. There is nothing to be done, as there is no one to do it.

Events unfold, creating the impression of cause and effect – what a convincing illusion!

In reality, sensations come and go... sights, sounds, thoughts, feelings... linked together by a mind desperate to make sense of it all.

The mind... what is it? A mental processor that labels and conceptualises perceptions. A storyteller. A fiction writer. It creates 'you' and 'me' and everything 'out there'. It scripts, produces and directs the movie of 'our life'. We star in the movie, alongside thousands of extras. The film seems to go on for years, featuring all types of dramatic episodes... love stories; tragedies; happiness; sadness... the whole range of possible experiences.

In reality, the movie is only ever appearing Now. Awareness of memories, future plans, and present perceptions: all are happening in the eternal Now.

This is the 'time of our lives'! Enjoy!

Feel around inside for the part of you
that is stopped in its tracks by the awe of simply being.
There's not a word that can be said about it.
This is it. This is love.
Already here, already yours.
Already you.
Enlightenment...
Nothing changes... life lived naturally.
Not special.

Suffering results from non-acceptance of what is. The desire for things to be other than they are is the cause of suffering. The mind (alias the ego) wants what it doesn't have; and doesn't want what it has. The ego is a chronic, neurotic grumbler… it is never satisfied. Why do we allow it to rule our lives, and cause all our unhappiness?

Because of mistaken identity. We assume the ego/mind to be who we are. The story of our 'lives' is believed to be real; instead of the fiction it is. The roles and 'personas' we adopt are assumed to be factual, rather than part of the drama being played out on the stage of life… albeit tragedy or comedy. We believe our thoughts, elaborating them into belief systems which control our behaviour and responses to life's situations. Why believe a thought, which has no substance or evidential reality? Why fabricate a total system of belief around a bunch of transient thoughts? "A tale told by an idiot – signifying nothing!"

The trouble is BELIEF. All types of belief. We believe in being a person; having a separate life to lead. We believe there are other people, objects, countries, religions. We believe what we have been told (or conditioned) to believe. We believe our opinions to be true, and will defend our beliefs (unto death in many cases). In short, we suffer because we believe.

Let us examine belief. Is it not the unquestioning acceptance of a proposition? Propositions consist of concepts. Concrete concepts such as table, car, tree, sky. Abstract concepts such as truth, love or God. Concepts are thoughts; albeit often elaborate thoughts. What are thoughts? We may think of an answer to that question, but that would simply be another thought. We might define thought as a wave of electrical energy within the cerebral cortex… but that doesn't really help, does it? We experience thoughts all the time… a continuous stream of mental activity; absent only in deep sleep. Thoughts arise unbidden; we know not what our next thought will be. They arrive and depart… where from and where to is a mystery. Thought sometimes provokes emotion; usually associated with memories or future speculation. Thoughts follow experience: e.g. we perceive a phone ringing and a split second later we are thinking about who might be calling. Essentially, thought is the past. It is made of concepts which have been learned and believed. Can you think of anything non-conceptual? Thoughts are conceptual and construct our image and knowledge of the world. We have constructed theories, made from concepts, which explain every question we can imagine. Thought will have an answer for most questions… science has seen to that.

But there are still certain questions that thought/science cannot answer. For example: "What is consciousness?" Modern science struggles with this question; but perhaps quantum physicists are realising that every aspect of energy is linked by consciousness… a force which is outside time and space. This self-aware consciousness contains and reflects all things. It **is** all things. The word "contains" is misleading; implying a sense of consciousness as a container. If so, there would have to be something outside the container; there isn't. Consciousness or presence or awareness (there are hundreds of terms for This) is **all** there is. *Advaita* (not-two). One-without-a-second. It appears as everything but in Itself is nothing… no thing. It has no purpose, plan or meaning. Seven billion specks of 'human' consciousness are appearing and disap-pearing continuously. Why?... we may ask. Any answer to that question will be another concept… another limited and incom-plete thought structure. So why bother to ask?

Relax into the Consciousness that you are. You are the energy of Life appearing for a while… dancing, laughing, crying as an actor on a stage… and then returning to the ocean of Oneness that in truth you never left. And don't believe anything!

Watching thoughts
Chasing other thoughts...
How tiresome!

How can we not be Awareness? Doesn't everything arise or appear within this Awareness? All sensations, perceptions, thoughts and feelings? If we become aware of these appearances, we must be other than them. We must be what contains them, and that has no form or dimensions; no centre; no circumference.

Awareness is normally directed outwards... towards objects, thoughts and sensations. Mind (which is more than mental habits) engages with and interprets these perceptions... labelling, classifying and judging continuously. If these outward perceptions are turned inwards towards what is perceiving, awareness becomes aware of itself. Attention is attended to... observation is observed. Witnessing of the show happens... without a witness. Observing without an observer... no separation. Everything apparently happening is Me... not caused by me (that would imply causality and subject/object division)... but IS me. Separation only arises in thought, creating concepts and objects. In the absence of conceptual thinking, how can there be any separation? All is part of everything else... and in the absence of phenomena, Nothing is Everything and Everything is Nothing!

The west wind strokes the elm
The Merlot strokes my throat
What marvels there are!

Awareness Training

Mysticism and belief systems are not needed. All that's necessary is awareness of awareness – paying attention to the Beingness that is Life. Sounds easy?

So let's practise paying attention!

Imagine attention as a muscle. Muscles need to be exercised to stay strong and healthy, so let's give your attention a good 'workout'.

Imagine your attention now as a camera, fitted with a powerful zoom lens, and also a wide-angle 'fisheye' lens.

(You may wish to close your eyes gently, and have someone read the following instructions out for you.)

First, aim the attention (camera) down your left leg, down through the knee into your left foot. Without moving it, or looking at it, what sensations do you notice? Pressure? Warmth? Zoom in further to your big toe – any sensation there? Keep your attention there for a while. If there are no sensations, notice that.

Now come back up the leg to become aware of the weight of your body on the chair. Notice the pressure and where contact is made with the chair and floor. Zoom back further and sense the contact between your clothes and your skin. What do you notice here? It may be a very slight and subtle touch.

Move your attention now to your breathing, without trying to change its rate or rhythm in any way. Just rest attention lightly on each breath, following it all the way in and all the way out. Perhaps noticing the momentary pause between each inhalation and exhalation. Relax and stay there for a while... simply watching the breath.

Expand your awareness around your breath now, to gain a sense of your whole body... sitting, breathing as a whole organism, relaxed, warm and peaceful.

Now direct your attention to sounds... sounds inside the room, and outside the room. Allow the sounds to come to you, and don't think about or label them... just be aware of them. Become aware of any smells or tastes that may be present. If there are none, then notice that.

Open your eyes and slowly look around the room. Don't label or think about what is seen... just notice the shapes, colours, areas of light and shade. Can you look at everything as if for the first time... like a young child?

Now think of what you did yesterday... what you had for dinner in the evening. Now recall the name of your first school, your mother's maiden name, the capital of Belgium. Imagine a green monkey; now an orange triangle... with green spots!

Remember an occasion when you were sad and upset... perhaps depressed and tearful. Can you contact those emotions again? Now a time when you were frightened or anxious? Sense those feelings... they cannot hurt you now. And now an occasion when you were really happy... filled with joy and excitement. Bring into awareness someone close to you who has given you unconditional love in your life. Imagine that person standing here in front of you, giving you their tender love and care. Feel that love in your heart... experience the power of that emotion.

Now, as best you can, imagine attaching the wide-angle lens to the camera of your attention; and allowing everything into your awareness. Welcoming all sensations, thoughts and feelings without focussing on, or staying with, any one in particular. Just an open, choiceless awareness... not labelling or judging anything. Everything appearing and disappearing in the ground of awareness. Noticing how all things are moving and continually changing.

Finally, and as well as you can (as this can be tricky), slowly turn your attention around 180 degrees, from the outside world, to look inwards. In other words, pay attention to awareness itself. It may be that you notice nothing... literally no-thing. Anything that does seem to arise is another thought… another sensation or feeling… arising within awareness. Some thoughts and feelings will feel 'sticky' (a bit like Velcro), may hang around and be difficult to shift. Other thoughts slip away quickly (like Teflon).

You may discover that **everything** arises within awareness; is contained by awareness. But awareness has no qualities or characteristics, and cannot be described, analysed, or known. It is the Source of all… it contains all. It is what you really and truly are! It is your true Nature… your Home.

So by simply paying attention to awareness, we can rest in an unchanging place which is outside thought and sensations, time and space, but which contains (and expresses) all of these things.

Where should we look for truth?

Where things never change – upstream of all appearances and concepts.

Even looking can involve concepts; of what we are seeking… of who is seeking… why… and on and on.

Non-conceptual awareness is simply resting in our true nature, which is Presence-Awareness.

It is turning attention around 180 degrees to rest upon what is always available; always in view if we care to notice.

Attention can give rise to concepts if the mind interferes; however, 'bare' attention is simply that – observing without any mental activity. So what is a concept? It's the mind at work… perceiving, interpreting, classifying and judging.

As you read these words the brain is instantly interpreting and translating them into ideas and concepts. The mind (which is simply a highly organised collection of concepts) creates meaning from the words, and then usually comes up with another question, or an objection. "Yes… but…" and so the intellectualising continues… and achieves nothing (except perhaps a headache!).

Warm bed
Cold feet
Everything just as it is!
Why chase 'happy'?
You get happy and then you get sad again, and what
    changed?
Stop chasing after 'happy'.
Right here, nothing changes.

Awareness is not 'yours' or 'mine'… it is Absolute. What does this mean? The Absolute has no limits, cannot be defined, known or understood. It is that within which all definitions, knowledge and understanding arise. It seems as if the Absolute imagines Itself to be a person separate from the world. This separation occurs in order that the Absolute can view itself, but in reality there is never any division. Only a pretence, a game of hide-and-seek, which fools 99.99% of humanity. A few 'individuals' discover the game, and see that the persons they thought they were never existed (except as illusions).

'You' and 'I' are One… the source of all objects that arise in the Awareness that we are. We are the Witness of all appearances that come and go; resting in infinite stillness and joy. Even the witness finally disappears into this silent brilliant space. We know that we are; and can state, "I am" with the confidence of Truth. Whenever we go further into conceptual thought, and state, "I am this or that", we move away from the Truth (which cannot be stated). The Absolute cannot be divided into 'this' or 'that'. There are no objects, because there are no subjects. Yet we cannot deny that we exist… that we Are.

Sunshine on flowers;
Birds singing;
Tiny tadpoles swimming;
The warm wind on my skin;

All phenomena arising within awareness,
Nothing personal... all Absolute.

The mind is a bundle of thoughts; and those thoughts have created the 'I'. Thought has created the object (*the world… everything 'not me'*); and the subject (*'me'… the little self*). Thought has also created Time and Space – those two concepts that underpin this illusory phenomenal existence. Thought has been busy! But what is thought? There is awareness, this backdrop of consciousness that undeniably exists. Against this backdrop, thoughts, feelings, and sensations arise. Continuously appearing and passing away; all the time that consciousness is present. In dreamless sleep this parade of perceptions ceases… 'we' cease to exist, so does time, space and all phenomena. All is absorbed within the 'Noumenon'… the Absolute… the fertile emptiness – the nothingness which the little ego dreads.

So again… what is thought? Is it a form of energy – a movement coming out of stillness? Like a pebble dropped into a silent pool… causing ripples and subsequent feelings, sensations and a train of associated thoughts? The energy of thought can be detected as electrical activity within the brain. Is the brain acting as a transmitter or receiver of these signals? Where do thoughts come from? Do we know what our next thought will be? Thoughts and feelings affect the thoughts and feelings, that is all. A thought, then a feeling arising, then another thought, then a feeling, then a thought… They affect each other but nothing else; they are just what they are, thought and feeling appearing and disappearing. You don't need to do anything with them… they come and they will go. Just see them for what they really are… just waves on the surface of consciousness. Just mental events… electrical activity in the brain. Nothing substantial or real.

I have no idea what's going on, ever.
I have no idea what to do next.
I have no idea what anything means.
I'm just vacant, and there's nothing here but bliss.
I don't even know who I am.
You don't know who you are either, but you're still too
    smart to see that.

Visitors

Can we simply rest in the miracle of being? Without the interfering mind seeking meanings, purposes and goals? Isn't THIS enough? The sound of Bach, the soft cushions at my back, the gentle spring sunlight... all these perceptions... and more. Surely nothing more is needed. And yet... the subtle pressure to 'do', to be active... achieving... accomplishing... this is also present. Memories of jobs still to be completed; tasks outstanding – all arising in this moment. All invading the peace and stealing the silence; when given attention. That's the secret! Whatever is given attention becomes our reality. Sounds, sights, thoughts, feelings... All competing for attention. Like a crowd of visitors all jostling around in my lounge.

Let's look at these visitors a little more closely. The first two visitors are small and look insignificant, but the gifts they bring are special. The first carries chocolate, which has a delicious taste. The second carries a bunch of roses, which smell wonderful... a delicate and subtle fragrance.

Next in the door is a musician, playing entrancing and exciting melodies, to which one could listen for hours.

But look! In comes a fantastic sight... a figure wearing multi-coloured costumes; shimmering in light and a rainbow of colours. The vision is so striking and awesome that the other visitors fade into the background.

Suddenly, the ground is shaken by the arrival of the next visitor, and a shiver of anticipation runs up our spines, and speeds our heart rate. In she/he rushes, and embraces us with fierce passion. We experience both pleasure and pain... the sensual cuddles and fondling and stroking grow into increasingly unbearable tickling, pinching and poking.

Comfort has been stolen, and both our skin and internal sensors plague us with a range of sensations. Experiencing heat and cold, pressure and pain, confusion reigns as our five visitors compete for our attention.

Our sixth and final visitor is uninvited, though barges through the door as if he owns the place. Huge and intimidating, he wears several badges... reading: "The Boss"; "Me"; and "Ego" – amongst others. From an inordinately large head, orders, explanations and requests are relayed. "I can explain everything!" he confidently claims; and starts to label and judge the other five guests. Somehow, once given a name and description, each of our previous guests' presents fade and lose much of their magic. They appear overshadowed by the bullying presence of our last guest, and sit around the edge of the room, vainly trying to attract our attention. As soon as one of them has entered our awareness, in comes our 6th visitor with a comment, critical or otherwise. We notice that this 'Boss' or 'Ego' carries several heavy bags labelled "memories"; "knowledge"; "fantasies"; "feelings"; and so on.

Every few seconds he takes a present from one of his bags and throws it to us, as if feeding a hungry pet. Often he takes a 'feeling' from his bag at the same time, and so perhaps a memory and emotion arrive simultaneously. Either a positive or negative reaction arises, either desire or aversion catch our attention. Powerful hooks grab our attention as thought after memory after feeling arrive in quick succession. Our last visitor declares himself to be "Mind" and claims to be who we are. His activities are hypnotic and he tries to capture and imprison us in the room. Indeed, despite the occasional pain (both physical and mental), we seem mesmerised by this magic show. We could lose our self in this performance, and forget who we really are, and what is real. Choosing to leave our guests to entertain themselves, we move to another room. Here there is nothing... simply emptiness in which our awareness can rest. No sensations, thoughts or feelings... just perfect stillness. Attention watching itself.

This is our true home; and although we can go back to the

'busy room' and join in the pantomime again, we know we don't belong there. We can instead rest here in the silence of our Heart. Peace. The cloudy water settling into clear beauty and Life simply Being. This cannot be communicated. Silence arises.

In dreamless sleep we are in another 'room'. In fact we are nowhere... and everywhere. We become aware of the contraction of the 'busy room' when we dream and when we 'wake up' into our 'daydream'. Once again we have the burden of 'I' and 'other'... subject and object... to contend with. Divided from everything, the mind protects its identity through falsely imagining the story of 'me'. Memories create a sense of continuity where in reality there is none... the universe is constantly new and spontaneously created in this moment. Mind has constructed 'time' in which to place the past and future; and also 'space' to separate things between 'here' and 'there'.

An elaborate and highly effective illusion. So strong that our conditioning prevents the 'seeing through' of this veil of deception. A glimpse of truth is immediately grasped by the mind, and explained away in conceptualised thinking. The mind cannot function without concepts, ideas and images; and thus cannot comprehend Reality. The Real is beyond concepts – upstream of mental activity – in fact contains all mentation. The Ground of Being is pure awareness, which contains all phenomena – physical, mental and 'spiritual'. Phenomena – 'appearances' – are inevitably limited and conditional. These constructs are of value only in the world of relativity – but are of absolutely no value in attempting to comprehend the Infinite. By definition, the Infinite cannot be objectified or conceptualised. So how do we approach it?

Any approach is a movement away from what IS – here and now. Any desire for the Truth should be investigated for its motives. Is it the desire for spiritual advancement; for personal enlightenment (*an oxymoron!*)? Is the ego subtly at work? No person has ever been enlightened, nor ever will be. For Truth to be realised, the person must disappear. Indeed, as an illusion, it was never there in the first place. A waking up from the dream of separateness is all that's needed, and the mind can't do that. There is nothing to **do**… and no one to do anything. So-called 'spiritual practices' may or may not happen… whether they increase the chances of 'waking up' is open to debate. Perhaps the only advice can be to: "Seek the unchanging – dismiss everything else."

When the One becomes many
There is lost an innocence,
Falling through the air like a heavy feather.
When the many appear as clouds of foes,
We lose ourselves in otherness.
The music drifts closer
Once the mind doesn't engage in judgment.
The light from the window embraces
Once the curtains disappear.

Tasting chocolate,
Hearing Mozart,
Looking at roses...
This is how I shall die.

When you wake up from a dream in which you've been late for an appointment; or involved in an accident; or some form of conflict… don't you breathe a huge sigh of relief and think, "Thank goodness that was not real"? We recall how vivid and realistic the dream seemed; how caught up emotionally we felt; and how these emotions affected our actions. We see that it was only a dream, and let it go. If we had dreamed that our house was on fire, would we call the fire brigade upon waking? It would seem ridiculous to carry on pretending it was real, and continue to imagine ourselves in an unreal situation.

So it is with our waking life… it is just another form of dream. A very realistic dream of being a separate individual in the world; very plausible but in essence an illusion. No more real than the scenes unfolding on our TV screens. Our very own soap opera, with our role being played so earnestly that we have totally forgotten that it is only a play. It can seem like a tragedy at times; at others a comedy; but the drama is always compelling. It compels us to take our roles so seriously that we forget we are just acting… we are not who we think we are. So the dream… the game… the play… continues until maybe we start to wake up and see the drama for what it really is.

Sensing the falsity of the play, some people seek a way to wake up fully, and assume a new role – the spiritual seeker. This is a very serious and dedicated role, but it keeps the 'person' firmly in the drama. The mind, which is responsible for producing this charade, is now expected to demolish its own production. Of course, this won't happen – a new, more sophisticated, identity is created instead.

Don't construct more 'selves'… see them all for what they are – creations of thought and the product of conditioning and 'education' (learned ignorance). Let them all go – and **be who you are!**

… And so you ask again: "Who am I?"

… And any answer that appears is a concept… a product of

the mind… another thought.

Can you let that thought fade away? And the next one? Can you allow all the thoughts to come and go; leaving the question unanswered?

The answer is to be found in the space – the silence – between thoughts. Nothing conceptual; nothing definable; no-thing. Not even a concept of nothing!

Then all that is left is this: a blustery summer's day… the sound of the wind on the windows.

The trees straining.

The birds swooping against the racing clouds.

This… sensing… thinking.

Only This… here… now.

The perfection of imperfection… and all too simple for words.

Words get in the way of true seeing. Can we see a flower without thinking about it? Without labelling, judging, comparing and analysing it? If we can, and then expand that choiceless awareness to all that we are conscious of… there's no more to say!

Is there a Way?

You may now be asking: "What can I do now? How do I achieve this insight/enlightenment/realisation?" Krishnamurti once stated that: "*Truth is a pathless land*" by which he meant that there is no particular method or practice to follow. Asking "How" implies a method, a recipe for liberation... just follow these instructions and you too will become a sage. This is a trick of the mind, which regards this as something new to get, something to boost the ego, a fresh possession. What has been written about here is not something that can be gained or achieved... it is already present in its fullness. We just don't recognise its presence. It is as if the pure open sky of the Real is obscured by clouds of thought. All that is required is to look beyond the clouds of conceptual thinking to discover what you were all the time... you are what you seek. You may think that you are a prisoner of the mind... but the door of this prison cell is not locked... it is wide open if you care to look. You already are what you are seeking. The Oneness you are looking for is Oneness looking.

So there is nowhere to go... moving anywhere is leaving what is. The question of practice is paradoxical – you have everything you need, but simply don't realise this. What is required is the removal of ignorance in order to recognise what was always there. There is nothing to gain except Self-knowledge. Perhaps for seekers there is a need to have pointers toward the truth, and so here are three of them:

1. Everything is a mystery.
2. There is no separation.
3. Nothing needs to be done.

That about sums up the world's wisdom. Within those three

statements is all the teaching that any sage can offer. We can teach ourselves… we do not have to join a group, adopt a belief system, or follow any guru or teacher. Exploring these three truths with our minds will lead us to abandoning the mind, and if we can do that, then freedom is ours… yours and mine! Consciousness freeing Itself.

If these three statements are not self-explanatory enough, let me elaborate:

1. Everything is a mystery.

What do we *really* know? Take fire, for example. We can explain the causes, types, influences and effects of fire. We can even attempt to define fire. But do we actually know what fire is? The simplest 'thing' needs words to explain it (other words themselves). All words are based on concepts and ideas… the concept 'table' exists only as a mental construction. Even if you argue that a 'table' exists as solid matter independently of the observer, this assertion can be logically dismantled on closer inquiry. Take away all our words, concepts and ideas. What is left? Immaculate perception? Seeing without knowing. Experience prior to mental activity. Awareness without interpretation. Claiming to 'know' anything is a conceit; a game we play with ourselves, deluding us into a sense of control and security. The reality (which is of course uncomfortable to admit) is that 'knowledge' is pretence, an illusion, and a 'confidence' trick. It gives us confidence… a belief that we can investigate, understand and thus manipulate our world. We can cause events to happen, predict phenomena, and assume command of 'our lives'. What arrogant nonsense! The unpalatable truth is – we know NOTHING… and as a result EVERYTHING is a mystery. We have created 'things' through thought… and we have no idea what thoughts are, where they come from, or how to control them.

Upon closer examination, thoughts are as substantial as soap bubbles, and just as important or significant. How foolish, therefore, to assume that the products of thought are any more substantial or real. They are no more real than the contents of a dream, and the product of a fevered imagination. So, let us be honest in accepting that we know nothing.

2. There is no separation.

The mind (as thought) divides experience into subject (the experiencer) and object (the experienced). This is a fundamental error. There is simply *experiencing*. Thought is inevitably dualistic... it splits Life into 'things'... labelling concepts, ideas and phenomena. It separates what is naturally One into many apparently independent parts. The action of the mind (merely a series of habitual thoughts) is to create a sense of being separated from the world, trapped within an apparent identity, name and 'personality'.

This illusion of separation is unreal, and the cause of human suffering and conflict. In reality, everything is interdependent and a facet of the Whole. The phrase used by Thich Nhat Hanh: "inter-being" is apposite here – everything exists in relation to, and because of... everything else. The ultimate reality is non-dual (*advaita* = not-two), a fact which the dualistic mind can, and never will, comprehend.

Is there any difference between the oxygen in the air, and the oxygen in your body? Between the water in the sea and the water in your body? Aren't these substances constantly being exchanged and moved around and between apparent individuals and their environment? If everything is one with all others, all distinctions simply fall away. All differences become meaningless... all divisions futile. The concepts of time and space (the products of separation) are seen through... understood as artificial constructions. There is no there and then... only Here and Now. Without a future, no goals are needed and seeking fades away. Whatever is sought has already been found… all targets already achieved. All that arises is part of one Awareness… one living presence that embraces all… IS all. Nowhere to go… nothing to seek. Perfect shining peace… just THIS.

3. Nothing needs to be done.

If there is no separation, then how can one move from 'here' to 'there'; from ignorance to enlightenment? If the essential unity of everything can be seen, the need to become something else – the desire for change – simply drops away. If all is Oneness, where else can one be except Here; *when* else can one be except Now?!

The seeker looks for achievement and spiritual success in the future – "When I am enlightened/liberated/happier/at peace"… the list is endless. All desire is based upon dissatisfaction with the present… wanting things to be other than they are (even in very subtle ways). Recognising that all is available and present at this moment – and always has been – invites an opening and relaxation into What Is. We are what we seek. We are already Home. Everything that has apparently happened in the stories of 'our' lives had to happen. Everything happened spontaneously in the present moment, which is the only time we ever have. All we ever wanted or needed was freely available. We were so busy looking for the key to our 'prison cell' that we overlooked the fact that the door was open.

Does that mean we just sit down and do nothing? Give up?

It can mean anything. Seeing through the illusion of separation can result in any action… any response. However, previous conditioning and deeply engrained habits of thinking and behaviour can remain. When the power to an electric fan is switched off, it continues to revolve for a while longer. Nevertheless, if separation and the false 'self' are seen through and dropped as unreal, a sense of energy and ease can be experienced. Whatever happens, whatever thoughts, feelings and sensations arise… it is all OK. Actually, it's more than OK… it is PERFECT!

What we want

What do each of us want from life? Many say they wish for peace of mind, or happiness. Can the mind be peaceful? Isn't its nature to be restless, active, asking for and seeking answers? If we look for peace in the mind, aren't we just stirring up more concepts; 'disturbing the water' with question after question? Peace may be found in the clarity and stillness that lies behind or beyond the mind. The mind, after all, is nothing but a collection of thoughts. Indeed, we cannot attend to more than one thought at a time, so how can peace be a thought? If the muddy water of a busy mind is left undisturbed by thought, it settles into clearness, and therein lays peace. The peace that truly "passeth all under-standing".

Trying to reach peace, or to achieve a peaceful state, is just the work of the mind, and not only misses the point, but is also a waste of energy.

Who you really are!

So as we near the end of this short book, are you any nearer to knowing who you are? Are you still the story you have told yourself over the years… or are you more than that? The only truth that you can ever be sure of is that you ARE. The fact of BEING is undeniable – if you are reading these words, holding the paper in your hand, you EXIST. There is immediate presence… immaculately clear and obvious. You are already that clear and present essential being. How can you be anything else?

The conscious awareness that you really are – outside of time and space – defies any form of description. It just IS, and whatever appearances arise in this awareness have no effect on it whatsoever. We have discovered together in the pages above that you are not your body, sensations, thoughts or feelings. What is left is NOTHING... but also the capacity for EVERYTHING! You are a full emptiness... an impossible paradox, which our poor little minds struggle to comprehend. I invite you not to struggle with all this, but simply to 'come home' and rest in this wonderful awareness where true peace and love are to be found.

BOOKS

O is a symbol of the world, of oneness and unity; this eye represents knowledge and insight. We publish titles on general spirituality and living a spiritual life. We aim to inform and help you on your own journey in this life.

Visit our website: http://www.o-books.com

Find us on Facebook:
https://www.facebook.com/OBooks

Follow us on Twitter: @obooks